OUR PRESIDENT: BILL CLINTON

by Shelley Bedik

SCHOLASTIC INC.
New York Toronto London Auckland Sydney

Dedication:
For Bill, Sasha, Max, and Aaron—and Lucy and Daisy, of course!

Photo Credits
Front cover: © Martin Simon/SABA. Back cover (left) Arkansas Gazette/SIPA Press; (right) Sygma © Ira Wyman.

Pages 3 and 29: © Ralf-Finn Hestoft/SABA; pages 5 and 11: Arkansas Gazette/SIPA Press; page 7: Clinton Headquarters; page 9: Sygma; page 13: AP Photo; pages 15 and 25: JB Pictures © Bob McNeely; page 17: © Haviv/SABA; pages 19 and 31: AP/Wide World; page 21: Sygma © Rick Maiman; page 23: Sygma © Ira Wyman; page 26: Nina Berman/SIPA Press; page 27: JB Pictures © Mark Peterson; page 28: © Steve Liss/SABA page 32: AP/Wide World.

ISBN 0-590-47126-0

12 11 10 9 8 7 6 5 4 3 2   3 4 5 6 7 8/9

Printed in the U.S.A.   24

First Scholastic printing, January 1993

Bill Clinton was born in 1946. He grew up in a small town called Hope, Arkansas. When Bill was a young boy, Hope was the kind of place where everyone knew everyone else. People didn't lock their doors at night. Everyone felt very safe there.

Three months before he was born, something very sad happened to his family. His father died in a bad car accident. So Bill lived with his grandparents while his mother went to school to become a nurse.

Bill when he was about 1½ years old.

Bill's grandmother believed that education was very important. She read to him all the time. She even hung cards around his high chair to help him learn numbers. She did a good job teaching Bill. He could read when he was only three years old!

Bill's mother married for the second time. The family moved to a new town, Hot Springs. Soon Bill had a new little brother.

Bill, his mother, and his stepbrother, Roger.

When Bill was a teenager, he was an important leader in his high school and church. He got good grades and worked hard to help people in his community. Bill worked hard at something else, too. He practiced his saxophone until he played so well that he won first place in a band contest!

Bill is in the first row on the far left.

One summer, Bill was chosen to be part of Boy's Nation. He met many other kids who were interested in leadership and the government.

That summer, he met the person who was then the leader of the whole country. He shook hands with John F. Kennedy, the President of the United States! Bill's mother says, "That's when I knew Bill would grow up to be in government."

Bill Clinton shakes hands with President John F. Kennedy.

Bill thought he might want to become a doctor. Then he thought he would make his living playing the saxophone. Instead, he decided to go to Georgetown University in Washington, D.C.

When he finished college, he won a big honor. He was chosen to go to a school in England to study.

Bill Clinton still plays the saxophone for fun.

When he came back to the United States, Bill started law school. He knew that he wanted to become a lawyer. He also knew that he wanted to return to Arkansas. He says, "All I wanted to do was go home. I thought I would start my law practice in Hot Springs and see if I could run for office."

During the campaign, Bill Clinton stayed in touch with people by holding meetings in small towns.

When Bill was in law school, he met someone he thought was very special. Her name was Hillary Rodham. She was a lawyer, too.

Once, Bill and Hillary were taking a drive. Hillary saw a house she thought looked nice. Just a short while after that drive, Bill said, "Hillary, I bought the house you liked. So you'd better marry me. I can't live there by myself." And Hillary said yes!

Three years later, Bill was elected governor of Arkansas. He spent most of the next fourteen years trying to make education, health care, and the environment better in his state. He wanted more jobs and better roads for the people in Arkansas.

Governor Clinton and Hillary attend a special dinner at the White House.

In 1980, Bill and Hillary had a daughter. Bill says, "I was there when Chelsea was born. It was the most incredible thing I've ever been through."

Now Chelsea is almost a teenager. She says, "My parents taught me to think for myself. And they taught me to treat other people the way you would want to be treated yourself." She thinks her mom and dad are great!

So do lots of other people. In 1992, they voted to make Chelsea's father the President of the United States!

Before Bill Clinton became President, he spoke to people on TV and was interviewed for newspaper articles.

He took bus trips and stopped in towns all across the country. He told Americans what he would do if he was elected.

He said that he would fight to get them better
jobs. He told them he would make sure children
and grown-ups get the health care they need.

He promised that schools will give kids a good education and that he will work hard to solve our country's problems.

As our forty-second President, Bill Clinton lives in the White House in Washington, D.C. That's a long way from his first home in Hope, Arkansas. But Bill Clinton thinks it's the right place for him to be. That's where he can do the work he always dreamed of.

President Bill Clinton and Vice President Al Gore will work together to keep our country strong and safe, and to make our planet healthy.

President Clinton, Chelsea, and Hillary Clinton with the Vice President's family: son Albert Gore III, daughter Sarah, and Tipper and Al Gore.

32